Some Immigrant

John Robertson Henry

Alpha Editions

This edition published in 2023

ISBN : 9789357966610

Design and Setting By
Alpha Editions
www.alphaedis.com
Email - info@alphaedis.com

Contents

FOREWORD

This little book for Junior Home Mission Study classes has been written from the point of view of a New York City pastor. The races that have been selected for study are so chosen because the writer knows them at first hand through having labored among them in institutional and church work.

The book is an invitation to become acquainted with the immigrant and be his friend and good neighbor.

The thanks of the author are due the many writers whose works he has freely used, the members of his staff, and Miss Alice M. Guernsey for helpful suggestions, and the Rev. F. Mason North, D.D., for reading the manuscript and for valuable criticisms.

J. R. H.

CHURCH OF ALL NATIONS,
New York City, April, 1912

I
WHO ARE THEY?

"Dago," and "Sheeney," and "Chink,"

"Greaser," and "Nigger," and "Jap."

The Devil invented these terms, I think,

To hurl at each hopeful chap

Who comes so far over the foam

To this land of his heart's desire

To rear his brood, to build his home,

And to kindle his hearthstone fire.

While the eyes with joy are blurred,

Lo! we make the strong man sink,

And stab the soul, with the hateful word,

"Dago," and "Sheeney," and "Chink."

—*Bishop McIntyre.*

Since we are going to study about "Some Immigrant Neighbors," it is well to know just what we mean by the words "Immigrant" and "Neighbor."

Immigrant. The word Immigrant is confusing because it looks and sounds so much like the word "Emigrant," but they are quite different. An Immigrant is one who comes *into* a country, generally with the intention of settling there. An Emigrant is one that goes *out* of a country, with the intention of settling in some other land.

The people we are to study are the Immigrants who have come, and are coming, into America.

Neighbor. Every one knows the meaning of the word neighbor. A neighbor is one who lives near another, across the street, or next door, or maybe in our own village or town. If you live in a large city it is not so easy to feel that the people who live near you are your neighbors. It was much easier years ago, when all that are now cities were only towns and villages, and many cities now well known were simply prairie with waving grass and flowers, roamed over by bands of Indians and trampled by the hoofs of countless bison.

The word neighbor has a larger meaning than merely one who lives near another. There is a wonderful description of a neighbor, given by One who is the World's Good Neighbor. He tells of the traveler who found a stranger lying by the roadside, wounded and helpless. At personal inconvenience and expense the traveler cared for the half dead man, and continued his aid until the stranger was again able to care for himself.

We shall have gained a great deal from the study of this book, if we learn not only to look on these immigrants as neighbors, those who live near us, but if we seriously ask ourselves how we may be Good Neighbors to the strangers from across the sea.

The Neighbors to be Studied. We are not going to talk about all of the thirty-nine races of immigrants that are separately listed by our government, but only about four of them. Some one says, "I hope you will tell about the ones I like." Well, we hope before we are through you will like the ones we shall tell about, and we are sure you will, for you will be better acquainted, and it is wonderful how much more likable the immigrant is when you know him.

Numbers. Although we are to study only Chinese, Jews, Russians and Italians, 333,694 of these four classes of immigrants landed in America in 1911; 920,299, almost a million, landed in the three years last past, and that is a large falling off as compared with some previous periods. In 1911 the Jews and Italians numbered thirty-five out of every hundred that came. You see that while we discuss but four classes, two of these are more than one-fourth of all that come.

These numbers may suggest very little to us, but how they would have startled the fathers of our country. The warlike Miles Standish, or, in later years, the peppery Peter Stuyvesant, would have declared no such numbers could be brought across the sea in a year. The only ships our fathers knew were small wooden sailing vessels like our coasting schooners; the giant, floating hotels that we call steamships, that carry a big village every trip, were not dreamed of in those days. The sailing vessel took weeks and months to make the voyage; now we can reckon, almost to the hour, the time of the arrival of a great liner.

A Jewish Immigrant

A Little Maid of Italy

It might be well if these numbers did startle us more and if we better realized how great is this invading army of strangers, friendly as it may be.

Dislike of Foreigners. Many people do not like the immigrants simply because they are foreigners. This prejudice is as old as the world, and its origin is a most interesting study. Perhaps some high school boy or girl can give a reason for this early dislike.

"The reasons for disliking the foreigner in early times were that no one traveled much and there were no newspapers, consequently neighboring tribes, or nations, did not get to know each other. Nearby tribes were suspicious of each other and were much at war, continually robbing and killing. Every stranger was a possible enemy."

Yes, that is a good answer. Now, give a reason for present dislike of the immigrant.

"I have a reason," one boy says. "My father lost his job because an 'Eyetalian' offered to work for less."

Yes, I am sorry to say that is a very real cause of dislike. That is also war, although it is now called by a different name. To take a man's position, by which he earns his bread, or to steal a man's cattle, from which he and his family were fed, amounts to about the same in the end. Give some other reasons for disliking immigrants.

"They talk such funny English." "They don't dress like us." "They don't eat like us." "They can't play ball."

Yes, undoubtedly all these are reasons for feeling that foreigners differ from Americans, but are they good reasons for disliking the foreigner?

I saw a "grown-up" show this hostile feeling one day as I was passing along a crowded street on the East Side of New York. An American youth of about eighteen years of age snatched some fruit from the push cart of a young Italian of the same age. The Italian grappled with the young thief and was giving him a sound thrashing when a policeman, leisurely swinging his club, turned the corner. With one glance he took in the scene of the Italian-American war. Raising his club and shouting, "You Dago," he charged full at the Italian. The young fellow saw him coming and took off down the street as hard as he could run, dodging as he went the flying club the policeman had hurled. When the tempest had calmed I stepped up to the officer and said, "Officer, what did the Italian do?" "Do?" said he with supreme disgust, "he was a Dago." Evidently the sole crime of the Italian consisted in being a "Dago," a foreigner.

To some people all Italians are either Dagos, or Guineas, all Jews are Sheenies, all Chinese are Chinks and all Russians are Owskies. They are foreigners, and that is enough. Such people forget that while the language of the immigrant sounds "funny" to us, ours sounds just as strange to him. While we laugh at the pig tail and queer shoes and strange clothes of the Chinese, they follow the American in crowds through Chinese cities and make fun of his absurd dress, and call him names that are not wholly complimentary, all because he is a stranger to them.

Our Debt to the Foreigner. It will help us to cultivate the spirit of a Good Neighbor if we remember that we are hopelessly in debt to all these foreigners.

Our Debt to the Chinese. The Chinese invented the mariner's compass that enables the sailor to strike boldly out into the deep, sure of not losing his way across the trackless ocean when stars and sun are gone. He is likewise an example to all the world in his reverence and care for old age, for father and mother. A traveler recently returned from China says he has never seen old faces more calm and kindly than those he met among elderly Chinese farmers. They seemed to think of nothing but the welfare of others. The rights of the parent are such that any father or mother with sons or grandsons living is assured in old age of the best care the children can provide. Though the son may be fifty years of age and have a family of his own he will yet give his own salary into the hands of his father week by week. The father need not worry about the future as do many fathers of large families in our own land, hence the calm eyes and care-free faces among old Chinese farmers. The Chinese teach that it is an honor and a duty for the young to toil for those who are old.

"Honor thy father and thy mother that thy days may be long upon the land which the Lord thy God giveth thee," is an old command and promise. The Chinese Empire is hoary with age. Can one reason for its long life be its obedience to this command?

Our Debt to the Italians. An Italian, Columbus, discovered the New World. Who, then, has a better right to inhabit it than his own countrymen? An Italian captain, Verrazano, was the first man to push the prow of his ship into the harbor of what is now the greatest city of the new world. Roman law rules the world and her treasures of art and literature have enriched every nation on earth. What school boy would like to be without the story of Julius Caesar, or not to have heard of the cackling of the geese high up in the Capitol the night the city was in danger, and how that cackling awoke the citizens and saved Rome?

Our Debt to the Russians. As to the Russian, it is an ungrateful American who forgets the service rendered this country in that saddest war of history, when brothers of the North and South rose in arms against each other. France had determined to found an empire in Mexico. She knew that this could be done only after the American Union had been destroyed. Russia refused to join with France and England in the course that might have made possible this division of our country. In the darkest days of our struggle the Russian fleet appeared at American ports as a pledge of her friendship and a protest against the attitude of these European powers.

Our Debt to the Jew. If we said nothing more than that through the Jew has come the Bible, that gift would place all of us forever in his debt. No other sacred book tells us so clearly of God; no other book shows us so truly how we may obey Him and be useful, strong, and holy. In no other place are we told the secret of that

"City builded by no hand,

And unapproachable by sea or shore,

And unassailable by any band

Of storming soldiery forever more."

It is true some of the Jewish people did oppose Christianity, but other Jews were the founders of the Christian church.

Through the Jewish nation came our Lord. Upon the streets of Jewish cities "walked those blessed feet that nineteen hundred years ago were nailed, for our advantage, to the bitter cross."

Kind neighborliness to these strangers is one way of repaying our debt.

———————————————————————————

II
WHY DO THEY COME?

Lo, the tyrant's days are numbered,

Liberty no longer slumbers,

Error dark no longer cumbers;

Risen is the Sun.

—*H. A. Clarke.*

MIGRATION. Why do such vast armies of human beings leave their homes? Why do they travel weary miles over land and sea and suffer such hardships and privations? The causes would indeed be urgent that would induce us to take a like journey and leave behind our pleasant, comfortable homes. Can it be that the home of the immigrant is not pleasant and comfortable? As we continue our study we shall find at least some of the reasons for this greatest migration in history.

On a beautiful day in autumn you may have seen large flocks of swallows wheeling around the steeple of some old church—"a river of winged life." Some one has told you they are gathering before they migrate. "Oh, yes," you say, "they are going away because they do not like the cold winter." In the spring, you have seen a great moving V in the sky all made of birds, and some one has cried out, "There go the wild geese," and you are told that they are journeying to the far, desolate North where the summer will soon be and where no one will molest them while they rear their young. So when great companies of people migrate there is a good reason. No one wants to leave a comfortable home without good cause.

You will be interested to study the causes of some of the great migrations in the past. If you will turn to the Book of Exodus you will find there the story of a vast human river of slaves flowing out of Egypt, across the Red Sea, into the wilderness. Why did they migrate? What drove the Goths down into the pleasant valleys of Italy? Did the richness of the Italian cities, the fertility of the plains, and the indolence of the inhabitants have anything to do with it? What brought the Tartars into China where as Manchus they have ruled 300 years, and where their long rein is now ended? The answer is simple. The Manchus were warlike Tartars, soldiers of fortune of a barren country. The Chinese were peace-loving dwellers in fertile valleys and plains. The better soldier was the victor.

There is no great nation of ancient or modern times but can tell its own story of migration. There once crossed into England a company of many thousands of splendid craftsmen bringing from France the secrets of trades that have helped make England great. What drove these Protestant families from their beloved land? There rang in their ears the solemn tolling of a great palace bell. That bell, sounding over the city of Paris, was the signal for the death of over forty thousand of the noblest Protestants of France. The St. Bartholomew massacre caused the migration.

In recent years a great tide of Irish began to move across the Atlantic. In ten years this mighty tide totaled over one million and a quarter human beings. The reason they came was the failure of the potato crop. The potato was their great food staple, as bread is ours. Great armies of Germans began to come after 1848. It would be interesting for you to find the reason of their coming. How hard it must be for the Southern Italian to leave his beautiful home and exchange his blue skies and hills and mountains for a dark, ill-smelling tenement, or for toil far underground in a mine. Why does he migrate and in numbers so great as to form every year a city the size of Portland, Oregon? We may find the answer farther along in our studies.

"If I were a Russian," some one says, "I would want to leave home. The winter is so long, there is so much ice and snow, I would be glad to get to a warmer country." But the Russian loves his winter. He drives his *sankey* with its hoop of tinkling bells arched high over his horse's back faster than any other horseman in Europe. In his home is a great brick oven and on top of this the family sleeps, no matter how the storm blows, as warm as a Negro boy in a Southern cotton field. The Russian does not leave his home because of the winter.

WHY THEY BECOME OUR NEIGHBORS

Opportunity. Some one says another name for America is "opportunity." Amid weeping and "*Il Signore vi Benedica*," "God Bless You," Giuseppe has gone away. He has been earning as *contadino* (farmer) 20 cents per day and is like a serf tied to the land. He earns in America $1.50 a day, or as much in one day as he earned before in seven. Giuseppe is frugal. He rises in his position to better pay, spends little money, and his bank account goes up until he has a sum that would have seemed a fortune in the little Sicilian village. Then, work slacking, he returns home. His watch and ponderous gold chain, his stylish American clothes, an exhibition of lofty independence, all make him a marked man.

Wherever you meet him on the village street, an awed, admiring group of friends is with him. He spreads the glowing tale of the New World and you may be sure the reality loses nothing in the telling. Every youthful heart is fired to a like adventure, to seek the golden, western world. As one returned immigrant said:—"It's a land where all wear shoes, where trains shoot through the air, and shoot through the ground; even the poor ride, no one needs an umbrella, the cars pass everywhere." It is little wonder they want to come. In America labor is dear and materials are cheap; in Italy labor is cheap and materials are expensive. There it pays a landlord to hire a man to watch his cows, rather than to build a fence, wood is so costly. In America no one would think of hiring a man for such a purpose, labor is so high.

The price paid in health and suffering for the money they take back is often far more than its worth. Many a poor fellow pale and haggard with that dread disease, tuberculosis, goes home hopeful that his genial skies will cure him of the death-blow the wet and cold and exposure of America have given him. But the defeated come home in the twilight, unattended and silent, while the successful swagger in at noonday with the blare of trumpet and beat of drums. As one Italian said to me no later than yesterday, "My uncle never told me the hardships I would have to face. I was far better off in Italy than here, but I am ashamed to go back." And yet, all who come realize that the possibilities of success are far greater here than at home. As another said, "In Italy I wanted to do but could not. In America I want to and can. I am sorry, but 'Good-bye, Italy.'"

The same opportunity for riches attracts the Chinese. He lives in a land that, labor as he will, is barely able to feed its almost half a billion human mouths. His wages at home are so meagre he can never hope for independence; two cents per day is what the farm laborer in Shantung earns. Since as a laborer he cannot legally enter the United States, he comes in under cover of darkness over the Mexican or Canadian borders, or any other way he can devise. The same hope of wealth attracts the Chinese.

Steamship Advertising. Many come because the steamship companies are such good advertisers. These companies paint beautiful pictures of the New World, and the peasant sees great farms, busy factories, and wealthy cities. The companies never show any views of dark, unhealthful tenements.

Through this steamship advertising many unfit persons sail for America, persons whom the agents might have known would be rejected, while many of the lowest class are induced to leave their country because their country is glad to get rid of them. It is said that in one small district in Austria two hundred and seventy criminals were released from prison one year and one hundred and eighty of them were in America within the next twelve months.

The Commissioner of Immigration at New York stated one year that 200,000 of the one million immigrants of that year were a real injury to the best interests of the country. Since the steamship company must be at the expense of returning an immigrant who is sent back, they make doubtful cases give a bond repaying them the return fare if the immigrant fails to slip by the "man at the gate." Of course the only interest the company has is to get the immigrant's money.

One steamship line anxious to make money brought over on one ship three hundred and eighty diseased peasants that Ellis Island promptly sent back. Among those peasants were many people of Montenegro. The Montenegrins are great soldiers. Tennyson wrote of them as

"Warriors beating back the swarm

Of Turkish Islam for five hundred years."

For five hundred years they have stood as a bulwark between the Turk and Europe. When they reached the home port, they stormed the offices of the steamship company, demanding the return of their fare, and after one look at their determined faces the clerks promptly locked themselves in and telephoned the authorities for help.

Some are induced to part with all they own, selling their little business and then, because of ill health or other difficulties that the agent might easily have known, are turned back broken-hearted and poverty-stricken to the village whence they came. Sometimes they are even sent to ports entirely different from those to which they had planned to go. This, of course, is all wrong.

The Employer. The reason back of the coming of many of these people is the employer, the man who manages the railways, the mines, or large contracts. He works through the padrones, and the Italian banks that "direct two-thirds of the stream of Italian immigration." You may be surprised to know that the news of a big railroad contract reaches Italy as soon as we hear it. If we are to build subways or barge canals, or carry an underground river into New York, or let great railroad contracts, or make a garden of the desert with colossal irrigation reservoirs and canals, the message flies under the ocean to far-away Italy and there is spread through a thousand villages.

The employer is constantly looking for cheaper labor. Around his mine or factory are American homes, practising the "American standard of living." This is a valuable term much in use and since it will occur again in this book we stop here to explain what it means. The American standard of living simply means the way most Americans live. Do you know that we live better than any other people in the world?

"I don't think *we* live well," one boy says, "we don't have an automobile, or a pony, or a piano, and the people next door to us do." But automobiles, and ponies and pianos, while pleasant to own, are not real necessities. Let us take a peep into the home of a Chinese boy. It is breakfast time and he is busy with a bowl of rice and a pair of chopsticks. Do you think you could eat rice with chopsticks? No! I think you would do much better with a spoon. "But doesn't he like milk and sugar on his rice?" Perhaps so, but neither milk nor sugar are in sight. Now, let us look in at dinner. Here are the same boy, and the same chopsticks, and the same bowl with more rice. "Where are the bread and butter, the meat and potatoes, and the dessert? We always have different things like that for dinner," you say. The Chinese boy does not seem to miss them; what seems to be troubling him is the small amount of rice left in the bowl.

Now take a look through this crack in the paper window, (the father of this little man is too poor to have glass windows in his home,) and see what our boy has for supper. Why there are the identical bowl, and the identical chopsticks, and what looks like the identical rice, though of course it is not. "So that is all this boy has had to eat for breakfast, dinner and supper— only rice?" Yes, that is all, and let me tell you he is very well satisfied, because he likes that much better than eating millet seed and that is what so many really poor Chinese live upon. As for shoes, our Chinese boy has none. His clothes cost only a few cents where yours cost dollars.

Nor is the Chinese boy so great an exception. The standard of living among the peasants in Russia is also very low; the same is true among the great mass of peasants in Sicily, and remember these peasants form the large majority of the population. That our standard is not the standard of living of some nations may be gathered from the question of the great Chinese viceroy, Li Hung Chang, when visiting America. After seeing the ever-present throngs of prosperous-looking people on the streets, he asked in great surprise, "But where are your working people?" He did not know that the happy-faced, well-dressed people he was looking at were working people practising the American standard of living.

The immigrant provides the cheap, unskilled labor. As he becomes influenced by American customs, he requires better clothes, a room for himself instead of sharing his room with ten other men, more pay as he becomes more skilled. He wants shoes for his wife. The American law compels him to send his children to school instead of making them wage-earners while little children. As his expenses increase he demands more money that he may live as the people about him live. Then the employer begins to replace him by labor costing what he formerly cost. Herein is a remarkable story that would fill many little books like this. It accounts for the procession of the Welsh, Scotch, Irish, Germans, and Huns in the coal regions. It accounts for practically all the civil war, in the form of bloody strikes, carried on in the Pennsylvania coal fields, and much of that which occurs in other industries throughout the country, this method of the employer seeking to replace those demanding higher wages by those willing to work more cheaply.

OPPRESSION

The Sicilian. Many come because of oppression in the home land. The Sicilian lives in a beautiful country, but while the sea and the mountains are good to look upon, the people are very poor. The farm worker cannot send his boy to school as boys go in America, for the rural schools are few. He must pay such heavy taxes he has little left for himself. Then, a few rich people own almost all the land and he must work for them, or starve. They pay him such small wages he cannot buy good, nourishing food for his children and they often suffer greatly in consequence. You draw a long breath when you are told his wages are from eight to thirty-two cents per day. Many of us use more each day in car-fare than a laborer in Sicily receives though he works from the time the top of Etna is crimson with morning, until the birds go to sleep. Even salt, so cheap with us, is taxed so heavily he cannot use it and when he cooks his corn meal in the salt water from the sea he is accused of smuggling. Oppression is what makes many of these people our neighbors.

The Jew. Let us step in and visit an old Jewish tailor, a saintly man who worships devoutly after the manner of his fathers. I am very careful not to give him any work on Saturday as it grieves him to disoblige his friends, and yet he will not work on his Sabbath day. He says, as do many others of the Jewish race: "I pray every day; my son prays once a week; my grandson does not pray at all." This old tailor speaks such broken English, we will let his daughter tell the story. "My father is almost eighty years of age; he never worked with his own hands until he came to America. He was for many years the tailor of a Russian regiment, making all the uniforms for the officers and having a number of men employed under him; we were well-to-do, the officers loved my father, but when the riots arose it was all they could do to save his life and all we had was destroyed. Now he is an old man, he should not toil any more, but," as she shrugs her shoulders, "who will give us bread?"

A kindly-faced man is sitting in my office. He speaks such good English you can tell he is a foreigner only by the peculiar way he pronounces some words. He says "dough" for though. Just imagine yourself sitting quietly by and listening, then you will know why many thousands come to us from one part of Europe. "We were friendly with all the people of our town. My ancestors had been in the same business for generations. All the Russians trusted us and although we were Jews they would rather deal with us than with their own countrymen. One day there had been many murmurs around us; the people had looked less friendly; they were ignorant, superstitious people, and they were miserably poor. Few of them could read or write. The nobility had fleeced them for centuries, but the nobility was too strong to be reached and so as scapegoats for the nobles we were pointed out as the cause of their wretchedness. We went to sleep that night, peaceful, prosperous and unsuspecting. At midnight our house was in flames. I never again saw father, mother, brothers, or sisters alive. I escaped in the night and was hidden by some friendly Russians. High above the roar of the flames and the din and slaughter rose the hoarse cry of the peasants—Our Daddy, the Tzar, wants it. Our Daddy, the Tzar, wants it." Multiply that scene by thousands and you have a Russian *pogrom*. Oppression brings many Jews.

The Russian. The Russian does not leave his land because of the winter cold. He leaves it because he dare not speak out against the wrong he sees. He is always fearful of some police spy making charges against him, shutting him up in prison, and sending him to Siberia. No one is safe from these spies. The Russian comes to America because here he can think aloud and here he can worship according to the voice of his own conscience. America is his hope.

One of our poets pictures America as she really is, a refuge for these fleeing, hunted people. He shows how the tyrant must give up the chase and return empty-handed when once these poor people have reached our friendly shores.

"There's freedom at thy gate, and rest

For earth's down-trodden and opprest,

A shelter for the hunted head,

For the starved laborer toil and bread,

Power, at thy bounds,

Stops, and calls back his baffled hounds."

III
OUR JEWISH NEIGHBOR

"O God-head, give me Truth!" the Hebrew cried.

His prayer was granted, he became the slave

Of "Truth," a pilgrim far and wide.

Cursed, hated, spurned, and scourged, with none to save.

Seek him to-day, and find in every land.

No fire consumes him, neither floods devour;

Immortal through the lamp within his hand.

THE NUMBERS THAT COME. So great has been the volume of Jewish immigration that the eyes of the country have been turned upon it in anxiety and question. In the ten years last past 1,012,721 have come. The largest number in any one year was in 1896, when 154,748 passed through the various ports. In 1911, 94,556 arrived. To better understand the meaning of these figures let us take a large map of the United States. Now be ready with a blue pencil and draw a circle around the cities I name. Perhaps I shall name the place in which some of you live. We will start with a city right on the Eastern coast of the United States, where you could step on board a steamer and sail away for Europe and see the homes of some of these people we are studying. The first city is Bridgeport, Connecticut, on Long Island Sound. The next is the capital of New York State, the city of Albany. The third city to get a blue circle is where a famous university stands, Cambridge, Massachusetts. Then we will journey away West and draw a blue pencil mark around the name of a city that stands near a famous lake out of which no one ever drinks. Yes, that is the name, Salt Lake City, Utah. While we are West we will mark Spokane, Washington. Then we will move South and place a circle about San Antonio, Texas; then come East to Reading, Pennsylvania, and Trenton, New Jersey. Michigan is a big state with beautiful forests, and we will blue pencil the city of Grand Rapids. One more city is needed to make the ten. If none of you lives in the cities I have named perhaps you may live in the last one we mark, Kansas City, Kansas. I hear some one say, "Why do you ask us to place a circle about these cities?" Because I want you to know that in the last ten years enough Jews entered the United States to make ten as populous cities as the ones we have just marked.

From Where Does the Jew Come? Five-sixths of the Jewish immigration comes from Russia. While the Jews number probably 11,000,000 in the world, about 5,000,000 of them live in that empire, mostly in what is called the Jewish Pale of Settlement. Why there are so many in Russia needs a brief statement. Poland invited the Jews to settle within her borders in order to build up her cities. Here was gathered the largest population of Jews since the destruction of Jerusalem. In some of the provinces of Poland the Jews number one-sixth, and in some of the cities one-half of the population. When Poland was divided between Russia, Prussia and Austria, fifteen provinces fell to the share of Russia. These form the Pale of Settlement, for there the Jew is allowed to dwell and there he is engaged in all forms of industry, including farming.

Why They Come. We have learned some reasons why the Jew leaves Russia. Other reasons are his desire for a better education for his children, freedom to engage in any business he may choose, and the privilege of worshipping God and of saying what he thinks without danger of arrest and imprisonment. Strange as it seems to us, there are still many places in the world where if a man thinks the judge or the ruler has done wrong he dares not say so openly. If he were heard to criticise them he would be in danger of prison. Sometimes when we complain of our own country we forget how fortunate we are to live in such a land of liberty.

Let us now find some of the reasons for the Russian hatred of the Jew. There could be no such merciless persecution of any race without some cause, and it is pretty well understood that the Russian government encourages and often provokes the attacks upon these people. The Russians dislike the Jews because the Jews are not Christians, and because they are much smarter business men than the average Russian, and would soon own all the land of the ignorant peasants if they were allowed to live among them and loan them money; the American Indian was cheated in this way by the smarter and better educated white man. Then the government does not like the Jew because the Russian government is corrupt and does not want the people to have a voice in governing themselves, and the Jew stands for the rights of the common people. Thus we see that while there is some just cause for dislike of the Jew, there are other reasons why he should be praised and commended.

As a Good Citizen. The Jew, having no country of his own has yet always been loyal to that of his adoption. The records show that when war came the Jew was willing to shed his blood for his adopted land. They are good to their own poor, providing hospitals for their sick, and homes for children who are without father or mother. The Bible tells us of the love of David for Absalom and the Hebrew king's prayer for the recovery of his little sick son. The Jew is no different to-day, he is kind and affectionate in his home. We know the evil the saloon does in every city and town and village in America where it exists. The Jew is generally an enemy of the saloon. The liquor business does not prosper where he lives. The Jews are lovers of books and education, and some of the greatest scholars, musicians, artists, and writers of the world have been Jews. Some of the noblest people who come to America are to be found among the Hebrew immigrants.

Not All Money Lovers. Jewish people are often accused of prizing money more highly than any other race and of setting a greater value upon it than they do upon either truth or justice. Some years ago a great strike took place in New York among the garment workers, who were mostly Jews. It lasted till the savings of the workers were exhausted. I was talking with one of the strike leaders one day and he produced a letter he had just received from his former employer. It said, "If you will come back I will make you foreman and double your salary." I knew the man was without any money, and I asked, "What will you reply?" "There is only one reply," he said as he tore up the letter, "I couldn't accept because I couldn't be a traitor."

The cheerful suffering that goes on among many East Side Jewish strikers is heroic, for they feel that they are fighting for principle and these battles that mean less food, thinner garments for the winter winds to pierce, and less fire in the homes, are fought with astonishing cheerfulness. In fact, it would be well for old as well as young folks to remember that the great battles being fought in these days are not with machine guns; these settle no principle. But the right to live, the right to live better than the brutes, the conviction that all one's time should not be required in the struggle for bread, for shelter and for clothes, that the life is more than meat, and the body than raiment,—for these things the Jews fight by enduring hunger, sorrow and even death for the sake of simple justice. They are the preachers of world brotherhood.

We do not mean that all Jews can be placed in this exalted class. Among them are the hardest and most merciless task-masters. Just the other day I heard a Russian complain bitterly because the Jews for whom he had been expelled from Russia were paying him the pitiful salary of $4.00 per week for his toil. But among them are a great multitude of noble men and women battling for a better day.

The Jew Intellectually. If I were to ask the question, "Are Jewish boys and girls at the head or at the foot of their classes in school?" I know the answer would be, "They are at the head." The Jew is delighted at the boundless opportunities for education in America. He is like one long locked out from a treasure which he could see but could not touch.

As a Business Man. As a money getter the Jew is without a peer in the world to-day; he seems to possess the golden touch we read of in the Wonder Book. But when we know how it is done there is little mystery about it. A Jewish family sent their children to my Sunday-school. They were poorly dressed and had the appearance of being ill-fed. After a year or two these signs of poverty disappeared and there was every evidence of comfort. I wondered what the cause might be and said to the children. "Your father is doing better, is he not?" "Oh, yes," they said, "he has gotten over the hard times he had when he went into business. He always used to get up at four o'clock in the morning and go to the factory and get the work ready before the tailors came. Then after they were gone he used to work until eight or nine o'clock every night, but he has a good business now and doesn't work so hard." Most men would succeed if they worked such long hours.

The Jew Spiritually. The Jew is a religious man but he seems to be losing his religion in America. In Europe the synagogue was a rallying point, in America the rallying place is the Labor Union, and many have turned away from the old faith. Family life, once loyal and beautiful, now shows many desertions, the father leaving the family to care for itself. The streets at night are trodden by too many Jewish girls, and the criminal courts are thronged with too many Jewish boys. Contempt for old age is one of the saddest products of American life. I have frequently seen young Jewish boys, twelve and fifteen years of age, mocking Jews as venerable as Abraham, both by pulling their beards and by sundry insults. The ignorance of Jewish children on sacred things is widespread. It is a question if any religious body has a more solemn festival than the Day of Atonement. It is supposed to be a day of fasting and prayer, but the restaurants are full, and numerous Jewish organizations use the day to make money by hiring a hall and selling the seats at a good profit to all who can be induced to buy. Many Jews who are members of congregations never attend service except on two or three of the principal fast days.

And yet, careless as the Jew may be of his old time religious faith, Christianity calls forth the bitterest opposition. He cannot forget the many things he has suffered in the name of the Christian church.

IV
OUR RUSSIAN NEIGHBOR

"Come, clear the way, then, clear the way:

Blind creeds and kings have had their day.

Break the dead branches from the path:

Our hope is in the aftermath;

Our hope is in heroic men,

Star-led, to build the world again.

To this event the ages ran:

Make way for Brotherhood—make way for man."

I mention the Russian not because large immigration has set in from Russia, but because I am personally acquainted with work among these people and because they are coming in increased numbers. When the Russian wishes to change his home, he is usually directed to some part of his own vast empire, and large numbers are settling in what was one time thought to be ice-bound Siberia, and are there successfully engaged in farming. There is, however, a constantly rising tide of immigration among the Russians. In 1901, 672 entered the United States. In 1911, 20,121, the largest number to date, was reported by the Commissioner of Immigration.

Intellectually. There is much ignorance among these newcomers. Over thirty in every one hundred who landed in 1911 did not know how either to read or write. A number of the Russians in New York are revolutionists of various classes; they are almost always led by the Jew, who acts as public speaker and general leader in most Russian affairs. About two-thirds of those who come are unskilled farm laborers and common laborers.

Religiously. While a large number of those who land are members of the Russian Greek Church, most of them are members of groups hostile to the church, although many of this latter class are unusually fine men. They are exiles from their country for causes that would often bring them honor in any really enlightened land. In fact, America has little idea of the great riches in heroism, sacrifice and splendid lives that are hidden away in the forbidding tenements of its great cities. The Russians' dislike of the church is deep seated and intense, for the Church of Russia has been the judge that sentenced them, the jailer that imprisoned them, the knout that whipped them. The Greek Church in many ways is an out-of-date church. It is an enemy of progress and free thought, the greatest ally of a cruel government. These men, knowing no other church than that of Russia, do not understand the difference between the Christianity found in America and this church of the Middle Ages in Russia.

One of the best loved and most influential Russians in New York City said to me recently, "My wish is to elevate my countrymen. Too many of them hold their club meetings in saloons and are given over to drinking habits. But I cannot have anything to do with the Christian church, for if I did I would be compelled to forget how the church has injured me and I have suffered too much from it to do that." The Jews share in this attitude of the Russian toward the church.

"Can any country afford to lose such men?" I put that question to myself as I looked over an audience of six hundred stalwart young Russians, their faces alight with intelligence, their whole bearing showing sturdy self-reliance, and yet lovable and teachable, withal. The place was an East Side hall, and the occasion a gathering to do honor to a Russian fellow countryman, and to enjoy a Russian play. The countryman was an exile because he wished to hasten the day of freedom for his beloved land. He was a man with a noble, melancholy face, and eyes that looked love and friendship. One wondered what that scholarly man could have done to have the sentence of death passed upon him.

The play when given in Russia was immediately suppressed, and yet it is founded on an actual happening. Imagine yourself with me at the Russian hall; let us take a seat and hear what the play is about and maybe we shall learn why it is that many Russians do not like the church. The players will speak in Russian, but we shall understand them for we shall have some one beside us to translate the Russian into English.

Now all is quiet. Here enters a young student in a red shirt and big top boots. He feels very important, for he has just arrived home from the University at St. Petersburg. His sister is with him. They are talking about a monastery in their village. "You know how the great monastery near us deceives the people," says the brother. "You know how the monks pretend the sacred *ikon* (image) on the altar works miracles, and how the poor peasants have to give the monks hard-earned money. You know how these cheats tell the authorities of any one who says he is dissatisfied with the government. And you know, too, that these monks are not good men."

"Yes," the sister says, "I am sorry that what you say is true. The monastery ought to be a great blessing to our village, but instead it is a great curse."

"Then," cries the student, walking up and down and much excited, "I am going to open the eyes of the people and show them that the monastery is a wicked fraud."

"How will you do it?" exclaims his sister, greatly alarmed. "Please do nothing that will cause the police to send you to prison."

There comes a knock at the door; the brother opens it, and in walks one of the monks from the monastery. He is such an unclean, repulsive-looking man you would want to run away from him if you met him on a lonely road. He does not look at all like the priests, or preachers, we know. He holds out a tin cup and whines, "Please help a poor friar who is begging for holy church." All the Russians in the audience laugh in derision when they hear the whining voice.

"Why is the church in need of money?" asks the student.

"We need money," whines the monk, "because the people no longer visit us as in years past, and since they do not bring money in we monks must collect it."

"But," persisted the questioner, "why have the moujiks stopped visiting you?"

"They do not believe in holy church nor in the sacred *ikon* as they once did." (The *ikon* on the altar of this monastery was believed to have worked many wonders.) "What the church needs is some miracle to restore the faith of the peasants," and the monk seems very sad, probably because he would rather sit down comfortably at home than walk the muddy Russian roads begging alms.

"Why do you deceive the peasants?" says the indignant student. "You know your sacred *ikon* never cured anybody, nor worked any miracle. I will give you the dynamite if you will blow it up." The monk admits the *ikon* worship is a fraud and says finally after a long discussion, "I will place the dynamite under the image and blow it up."

When the time comes to explode the dynamite, the monk is afraid and confesses the plot to the Abbot. "Let us blow up the altar," says the Abbot; "we can say the anarchists did it, but we will first remove the *ikon* and then tell the people a miracle was wrought—the altar was destroyed, but the image was saved."

The Home of a Russian Peasant

A Russian *Moujik* and His Family

So the altar is blown up after the priest has removed the image. The people are told it is a marvelous miracle and the church is crowded again, each peasant not forgetting to leave his copeck, half a cent, as he departs.

After the explosion, the student says, "I will go to the monastery and when the great crowds of peasants are coming out of the chapel I will tell them just how great a fraud the latest miracle is." So he goes and tells the people how grossly the monks are deceiving them and that it was his plan that destroyed the altar. Do the people believe him? Oh, no. They believe what the priests tell them and they are so angry with the young informer for saying he blew up the altar and for trying to open their eyes that they kill him.

"But," some one says, "we have been looking at and hearing only a play." Yes, that is true, but it is a true play, for all you saw actually happened in Russia, and it is the deception of such monks that has made so many Russians hate the church and hate God.

You noticed how the audience leaned forward in their seats, each seeing in that picture his own story, the forces that drove him far from his fatherland. You also remember what the interpreter said at a great burst of applause, the greatest of the night, when we asked, "What was that for?" "Why," said the interpreter, "you will be surprised to know what they are applauding. In reply to the question as to who was his most bitter enemy, the actor has just said, 'My greatest enemy is God; through God and the church come all my troubles.'"

It is the duty and the privilege of the Christians of America to introduce these Russians to a true church, and to instruct them in the knowledge of the true God.

V
OUR ITALIAN NEIGHBOR

"Genoese boy of the level brow,

Lad of the lustrous, dreamy eyes

Astare at Manhattan's pinnacles now

In the first, sweet shock of a hushed surprise;

I catch the glow of the wild surmise

That played on the Santa Maria's prow

In that still gray dawn,

Four centuries gone,

When a world from the wave began to rise."

—*R. H. Schauffler.*

NUMBERS. Our immigrant neighbor that has attracted the most attention in the last decade has been the Italian. He has attracted this notice, first, because of his great numbers and, second, because of the inferior quality as compared with much previous immigration.

Over two millions have come from Italy in the past ten years, and the numbers show little prospect of diminishing. This stream that two decades ago was but a tiny rivulet is now a human Amazon. The Amazon of South America pours so vast a tide into the ocean that the sailor while far from sight of land may yet dip his bucket overboard and draw up fresh water. We may well inquire about these people who are flowing in so vast a flood into the sea of our American life.

In the year ending June 30, 1911, 213,360 Italian immigrants entered. In 1910, 233,453 were admitted. The largest number entering in any one year was in 1907, when 294,061 passed through the various entry ports.

When we are dealing in millions figures suggest little or nothing to us. Let us take another method to show the large numbers of this one nationality that are pouring in through all our gates.

Imagine the two millions of the last ten years drawn up in a single line, each holding the hand of the fellow countryman on his right and left. How far will this human chain extend?

Suppose we step aboard a train at New York. We pass along the Palisade-bordered Hudson, past Yonkers, West Point, Poughkeepsie, Hudson and Albany, one hundred and fifty miles. These black-eyed children of Italy line the track all the way. At Albany we turn west and go to Utica, Syracuse, Rochester and Buffalo. We have come over four hundred miles and still the line is unbroken. Here the porter makes up our sleeping berth, and all through the night, past Detroit and into Chicago, the metropolis of the Middle West, along a thousand miles of railroad stretches our imaginary hand-clasped line. From Chicago we journey still further toward the sunset until we rumble across the Father of Waters and into the station at St. Louis. Surely these endless faces are no longer beside our train. But there they are; westward still extends our immigrant line. From St. Louis we travel right across the state of Missouri to Kansas City, almost three hundred miles. Our train moves so fast across the level country that the hand-clasped strangers seem like closely placed pickets in an endless fence, but still the line is there and we must travel one hundred miles across Kansas before the last of that endless chain waves us farewell. And all these have come in ten years.

The Italian Compared with Former Immigrants. The earliest immigration to America was not that of the peasant class. "It was the middle class tradesman and the stout, independent yeoman." The immigration of a few years ago, as is well known, was from Northern Europe, bringing the German, the Scotch, the English, the Irish, the Welsh and the Scandinavian. These were races from the temperate zone who had gained culture and the virtues of a Christian civilization, largely Protestant, through long centuries of intelligent struggle. The Italian immigrant of today is from Southern Italy. The Northern Italian, more skilled and better educated, does not come to the United States in any large numbers; his goal is mainly Argentina and Brazil, in South America.

The Italians from Sicily have lacked educational advantages. If, when they land at the Battery from Ellis Island, you asked them to read the name of the street upon the lamp post, sixty out of every hundred would shake their heads. In the public schools the Italian is by no means so clever as some of the other immigrants, nor is he employing his leisure time in so wise a manner as is the Jew, for instance.

Thrift. The Italian is frugal and thrifty. Most of them seem to have money. A poor woman exclaimed at one of our free Saturday night concerts some time ago, "O Signore, some one has robbed me." I looked at her and thought to myself, "She is so poorly dressed I do not believe she has lost much," but I said, "Come and see me after the concert." On talking with her I found that the thief had been better informed than I, for he had cut the skirt of her dress with a knife and had taken $80 which was in an inside pocket. It is no unusual sight for a laborer to draw from his wallet a roll of bills amounting to $50 or more to pay for a ten cent spelling book in our night school. The amount of real estate the Italians own in New York is very large; some years ago it was estimated at over sixty millions. It is probably more than double that today. Some of them own tenements and rent rooms that are slept in by day by one shift of men and at night by another.

One must be careful that he is not an innocent party to placing children in orphan asylums and other such homes to be educated at the public's expense when the family is entirely able to support its own children. An Italian woman wished me to place her two boys in "college." By "college" she meant an orphan asylum. When I investigated I found that she was married, had a husband who was in perfect health, and was herself worth between three and four thousand dollars. The church receives very little financial support from these people, although they are lavish enough when it comes to a big display at a wedding, a christening, or a funeral. The money paid for bands to walk before the hearse must amount to hundreds of thousands of dollars every year in the Italian colony of New York City.

How They Are Misused. There is no question but that the Italian earns the money that is paid him in America; no better laborers ever came to these shores, and the way they are sometimes misused is shameful. I saw once a pitiful exhibition of this. It was an August day, one of the most intensely hot I had ever experienced, and all the worse because it was in a long succession of stifling days and nights. Everywhere men were stopping their horses and cooling them off with the hose, or with pails of water and, despite it all, dead horses were lying in all the principal thoroughfares.

An Irish boss was foreman of a gang of Italians that was asphalting a city street. A line was drawn down the middle of the street and the force divided, each gang taking the part on either side of the line from the middle of the street to the curb. The gang that asphalted their half of the block first would receive as reward a keg of beer that stood perched, temptingly, on an elevated platform at the end of the street. I do not remember ever seeing elsewhere human beings driven at such inhuman speed; it was a cruel proof of what greed and a total disregard of the welfare of the poor immigrants could furnish.

A writer in "Everybody's Magazine" saw the statement of the press agent of the Erie Railroad that no lives had been lost in cutting the great open air rock entrance of the Erie into Jersey City. He was interested enough to investigate it, and he learned of twenty-five who were killed and so many who were injured that a partial list filled four newspaper columns, a year before the work was completed. "Why," he asked, "was it said that no lives were lost?" "Because," was the reply, "the killed were only Wops (Huns) and Dagoes."

Spiritually. The Italian is naturally religious, and when converted he becomes an earnest, intelligent follower of Christ. We must not fail to tell him the story of "Jesus and his love."

VI
OUR CHINESE NEIGHBOR

"Dago," and "Sheeney," and "Chink,"

"Greaser," and "Nigger," and "Jap";

From none of them doth Jehovah shrink.

He lifteth them all to His lap,

And the Christ, in His kingly grace,

When their sad, low sob He hears,

Puts His tender embrace around the race

As He kisses away its tears,

Saying, O "least of these," I link

Thee to Me for whatever may hap,

"Dago," and "Sheeney," and "Chink,"

"Greaser," and "Nigger," and "Jap."

—*Bishop McIntyre.*

THE MISUNDERSTOOD CHINESE. The Chinese are the most misunderstood people in America, and the reason is probably found in the Celestials themselves. No author in writing about this myriad people feels that he can give an account of the Chinese in one province, or city, or village, that he is sure will hold good in another. The earliest bit of wisdom concerning the Chinese that I remember acquiring was the statement in an old geography that to write one's name in Chinese characters was a sure way of winning their favor. I now know that I am no surer of winning the favor of a Chinaman by writing my name in Chinese characters than a Chinese would be of winning my favor by writing his name in English letters. But the writer of the old geography may have been acquainted with some place in China where what he states was true.

In our short account of these people we can catch but a fleeting glance, seeing little more than the curious Chinese himself, who, "when he wants to get a peep inside a house applies a wet finger to a paper window so that when the digit is withdrawn there remains a tiny hole through which an observant eye may at least see something."

Unchanging China. What force was back of the movement that reached its height in 1892, when almost 40,000 of these people landed in America? What caused the first large migration from China to the United States? Today very few come. In 1911 but 5,657 Chinese entered, while 7,065 went back to China.

That the Chinese would require some powerful force to set this tide in motion, a few instances would indicate. The Chinese do the same thing in the same way today as their ancestors did it five hundred years ago. If a village street is so crooked that one must walk an extra mile, no one would think of straightening the street. If the village well was the source of water supply in the past centuries, the substitution of a pump would not be thought of, as it would be an insult to the past. They dislike even the most trivial changes; the altering of the time of the regular hour of meetings; a re-arrangement in the seating of their class rooms, or the transfer of a teacher, all disturb them. Because things used to be done in such and such a way is the reason that they ought to be done so now.

Old customs are followed, although the life has long since departed from them.

For example, "It is the custom in Mongolia for every one who can afford it to use snuff and offer it to his friends. Each man has a small snuff box which he produces whenever he encounters a friend; if the person with the snuff box happens to be out of snuff, that does not prevent the passing of the box, from which each guest takes a deliberate, though imaginary, pinch and returns it to the owner. To seem to notice that the box was empty would not be good form, and all is according to a well settled precedent."

"In a country like China, which stretches through some twenty-five degrees of latitude, but in which furs are taken off and straw hats are put on according to a fixed rule for the whole Empire, in regions where the only heat in the house during the winter comes from the stove bed or *k'ang*, it is not uncommon for travelers who have been caught in a 'cold snap' to find that no arguments can induce the landlord of the inn to heat the *k'ang*, because 'the season for heating the k'ang has not arrived.'" American street car companies and apartment house owners have at times taken a leaf from the Chinese in this particular. What could move this people to leave their home and seek a new world?

THE CHINESE IN AMERICA

What Caused Their Coming? The first large migration of the Chinese to America may be explained by two words, War and Gold.

In 1850 the great Tai Ping rebellion broke out and soon spread poverty and ruin through southeastern China; the terrors of war with its ever present hand-maidens, famine and plunder, ruined all business and paralyzed all industry. The farmer class of the sea coast districts was driven into Hong Kong and there they met the astonishing stories of the fabulous wealth in the recently discovered gold fields of California and Australia. That, in brief, is the history of the first big wave of Chinese migration to America.

The Sort of Chinese Who Came. Those who came were largely from the farmer class. The Chinese farmer is very different from the Sicilian farmer; the latter rents his land at a ruinous price from the large land owner, or works it for a meagre wage almost as a serf; the Chinese farmer belongs to one of the most honored classes in China. "He owns the land, has freedom of trade and industry, local self-government, can appeal against official misgovernment and has the opportunity to rise to any social or political station." The social system of China is well worth keeping in mind. First in rank comes the scholar, the man with the trained mind fitting him to be a wise leader and guide; second, the farmer, the producer, the creator of wealth; third, the artisan, who changes the raw material into usable forms, makes furniture of the timber, pots from the iron, dishes from the clay; fourth, the merchant, the middleman, who sees to the distribution of flour, rice, clothing, etc.; fifth, the laborer; and last, the soldier or non-producer. In what order do we rank these classes? The early type of immigration from China was of a high grade.

How They Were Received. The Chinese were received in California with open arms, so to speak. "Industrial necessity" overlooked the visually present race prejudice, and the Chinese turned their hands to anything that would fill the gap the American gold-seeker had created. They became cooks, restaurant keepers, laborers, household servants—there were no women on the Pacific Coast then, willing to do the last named work—carpenters, farmers of neglected land. Governor McDougall, in 1852, recommended a series of land grants to induce their further coming; editors praised their industry, their cheerfulness, and personal cleanliness; the Chinamen must have thought the Golden Age was come again.

The Rude Awakening. In 1854 came the collapse of the California boom; placer mines gave out; men from the mines seeking employment were coming to the city in droves; the wage of $10 per day for skilled and $3.50 to $5 for unskilled labor was over; then came the cry of America for

Americans. The Chinese were ill-treated and many lost their lives. Committees were formed by the better class of Americans to protect them, but the cry against them never ceased in California until the Chinese exclusion law of 1888 was enacted, barring them from the country.

The Chinese Intellectually. The Chinese rank high intellectually. Their age-long reverence for learning—for a knowledge of the Chinese classics opened the door to the highest positions—has undoubtedly had a marked effect upon the mental side of the nation. The Chinese hero has been the one who passed successfully through the various examinations in the classics and finally, after many difficulties, attained the coveted degree. Their "highways are spanned with arches erected, not to great soldiers, but to great scholars."

The nature of the outings that the average young American of the East Side conducts is pretty well known throughout the city of New York. They are usually anything but orderly and thoughtful. But on a Christian Chinese picnic I have gone from the bow to the stern of the boat and found numerous games of Chinese chess in progress, each game surrounded by an excited group of advisers telling the players what move to make to checkmate their opponents. The playing of a good game of chess is not a childish task. The Chinese are a thoughtful people.

Generosity. Few favors done the Chinese pass unrewarded. I have seen many touching examples of sympathetic helpfulness. A few years ago a beautiful Chinese woman was helped to escape from worse than slavery. To save her from the sworn vengeance of her master, it was necessary to send her clear across the continent in company with a missionary. This we did. Like Nicodemus, who came to our Lord under cover of darkness, there came to us later a woman from Chinatown. Her husband is one of the most notorious gamblers in the country, but his wife had a woman's sympathy with the kindly service rendered, and she left a hundred dollars as her gift toward the safety of her unfortunate countrywoman.

Spiritually. I am repeatedly asked, "Do the Chinese ever become Christians?" Their spiritual nature is as keen as that of any foreign-speaking people that come to us. The spirit that changes the life of a wicked, gambling, drinking American performs a like office in a wicked, gambling, opium-smoking Chinese. The Christ that attracts little American boys and girls is a like magnet to these little Chinese lads and lassies. We had in our school for some years a little Chinese boy named Guy. He was bright and courageous, and accompanied our missionary on many of her visits among the Chinese. He said one day, with great earnestness, "There are three things I want. First, I want to become a Christian and get my heart right; second, I want to be baptized so that all the Chinese may know that I am separated from paganism, and third, I want to be a preacher of the Gospel so that many may hear the glad news." You will agree that these are good wishes for even an American boy. One night he dreamed that his father, who was in China, had returned to America and that he and Guy stood together at the altar of a church while Guy was being baptized.

Wong Sing came into our night school seven years ago. He hated the name of "Jesus." When he heard in America that Christ was being preached in his native village, he said, "Hot anger rose within me." One reason for this was that Wong Sing knew only the Christianity of Mexico, and this is cruel and disdainful toward the Chinese. It has taken the world many centuries to learn that the Christianity of Jesus is best extended not by sword or force, or even by argument, but by loving-kindness.

A Chinese Family

(Church of All Nations, New York City)

One day Wong Sing went home from our school with a Chinese New Testament, and to him it was the Word of God from heaven. He read it all night, getting an hour's sleep in the early morning before he went to work. He was converted by the reading, and then he threw himself, with all his soul, into the work of the church. He was all for Christ. In the last four years he was with us he did not miss one session of the school.

Finally, business called him home. His mother in China was greatly grieved at his conversion. She said, "My son has deserted the old faith. When I die, who will worship at my tablet? My son went away a good boy, he comes back possessed of a devil." Wong was the only Christian in the village. He tried to show his mother the better way he had found in Christ, but without success, and in great bitterness of heart over the loss of her boy's faith in the old religion, she ended her own life. On this young Christian has fallen the curses and revilings of the entire village, but he has "kept the faith."

When You Toy, a little Chinese slave girl whom we had rescued, told us her dream, we felt that there was a relation between it and her own life and thinking. "Oh," she said, "I had such a wonderful dream; I saw God and He had a great book, and He called me to Him and said, 'Here, You Toy, look in this book,' and I looked and there was my name, and after it in bright letters was written, 'You are my precious one.'" I believe that a little orphan girl from a far country, trained in ancestor worship, could never have had that dream if God were not a known and near friend. What do you think about it?

The Russians, Hebrews, Italians and Americans—none of these people surpasses the Chinese in loyalty and in labors, once they become followers of Christ.

VII
MAKERS OF GOOD NEIGHBORS

"Fear not, we cannot fail:

The message must prevail;

Truth is the oath of God,

And sure and fast,

Through death and hell,

Holds, onward, to the last."

TO BEGIN WITH. Who and what are the good neighbors in our country that are most powerful in changing this many-tongued multitude into Americans? Who are influencing them so that they understand us and we understand them? What forces are welding these many fragments into one nation?

To receive into one great common home millions of sons and daughters strange to that home and to one another in speech, custom and land, and to blend them into one people, this seems an impossible task. And yet it is being accomplished.

The Public School. Among the good neighbors that are grappling with this great task most effectively I place the public school first, because I believe it the most useful neighbor in making young Americans. Frequently the foreign-born parents see the New World largely through the eyes of their children, so that the school is a good neighbor to the whole family.

The public school makes different nationalities friendly. All school boys know how by studying together, reciting together and playing together they acquire respect for one another, and learn to look over the barriers of race. A public school near my church which is made up almost wholly of Jews and Italians, elected one of my Sunday-school scholars, a Japanese boy, president of the class, simply because his ability and good manners had won their respect.

Manual Training. By manual training classes the public school promotes respect for work with the hands. We cannot understand the foreigners' contempt for this kind of work, but it is very strong. I once took an Armenian, who had come all the way to America in the hope of getting an education, to the president of a preparatory school in the hope that he might be admitted free of expense by doing some work about the institution. The president stated that the school was overcrowded, but he would take him in if he would work in the field a couple of hours a day. The Armenian, who was really an earnest man, felt the work would too greatly degrade him, and declined.

Teaching in the English Language. The English language is of course another great help in Americanization.

The City and the Immigrant Child. The child of the immigrant is in special need of the help and sympathy of all American boys and girls. Frequently he is the sole person in the home who speaks English, and so is called upon for advice and is consulted in many things upon which American fathers and mothers never need to consult their children. This is unfortunate for him, as we can readily see. He often despises the language and customs of his parents and then ends by despising the parents themselves. He cannot understand the love his parents feel for their homeland; he cannot see the blue skies and green hills and mountains so dear to them; he cannot feel the home attachments.

"I recall a certain Italian girl," writes Miss Jane Addams, "who came every Saturday evening to a cooking class in the same building in which her mother spun in the Labor Museum Exhibit; and yet Angelina always left her mother at the front door while she herself went round to a side door, because she did not wish to be too closely identified in the eyes of the rest of the cooking class with an Italian woman who wore a kerchief over her head, uncouth boots, and short petticoats. One evening, however, Angelina saw her mother surrounded by a group of visitors from the School of Education who much admired her spinning ability, and she concluded from their conversation that her mother was the 'best stick spindle spinner in America.'

"When she inquired from me as to the truth of this deduction I took occasion to describe the Italian village in which her mother had lived, something of her free life, and how because of the opportunity she and other women had had to drop their spindles over the edge of a precipice they had developed a skill in spinning beyond that of the neighboring towns. I dilated somewhat upon the freedom and beauty of that life, how hard it must be to exchange it all for a two-room tenement and to give up a beautiful homespun kerchief for an ugly department store hat. It was easy to see that the thought of the mother with any other background than that of the tenement was new to Angelina, and at least two things resulted; she allowed her mother to pull out of the big box under the bed the beautiful homespun garments which had previously been hidden away as uncouth, and she openly came into the Labor Museum by the same door as did her mother, proud at least of the mastery of the craft which had been so much admired."

While it might seem that the child represents the most precious future wealth of our cities, he evidently is not so valued. Real estate is worth more than he is. Dirty, disease-breeding blocks that should be parks and playgrounds are worth more than he is. Even where grass grows, big signs everywhere indicate that grass is sacred and of more account than he is. In planning our American cities the child seems to have been entirely left out. When tenements became profitable, and the tenements are the homes of the immigrant children, the backyard playground disappeared. The street is the only playground left and, cursed by drivers because the horses stumble over them, and by chauffeurs because they limit their speed, and chased by the police as a general nuisance, the children of the tenements are surely to be pitied.

A young Italian girl fifteen years of age was being sworn in a Brooklyn court. Before swearing her the Judge told the clerk to inquire if she knew the meaning of an oath in court. He asked, "Do you know who God is?" She replied, "God, who is he?" He said, "Do you know anything about Christ?" She replied, "Christ, where does he live?"

Here is a chance for the boys and girls of America to be good neighbors.

The Settlement. Some one says, "I have often heard about settlements, but what do they do?" The Church of All Nations carries on a church and settlement work on the lower East Side of New York. If you were to pay it a visit during a week day this is what you might see. By 8.30 o'clock in the morning there would be a patter of little feet and a babel of children's voices and we would know the Italian boys and girls were coming for the daily kindergarten. At nine o'clock the office bell begins to ring; just sit in the office and listen to the people who call. One says, "I need to go to the hospital"; another, "I want to get a friend out of prison"; a big able man says, "I want work"; some are in need of clothes or food, or a lawyer, or are discouraged and have come to talk over their troubles. These last keep coming during the morning office hour and, in fact, all day and into the night.

Italian Kindergarten (Penn.)

In the afternoon there is a mother's meeting for Italians, or Hebrews, or some other nationality, with an address of a religious nature or a brief talk on some topic that helps make the mothers better able to care for their children. American boys and girls may think all mothers know how to take care of children, because their mothers took such good care of them. It would surprise them to know that in the fall some of the immigrant mothers sew a suit of clothes on their child and expect that suit to stay on through the winter—it is not to come off at night, either. Many Italian mothers wrap up their little babies until they look like a mummy that you may have seen in a museum. The baby can move its hands but not its feet; it can also move its big black eyes, and laugh or cry. We know better than these mothers, so we try to teach them wiser ways of caring for their children.

At three o'clock there may be sessions of the sewing-school, or game room, or gymnasium classes for the younger boys who are not allowed to come at night. In the evening there are club meetings under chosen leaders, bowling contests, basket ball games, and night school for Italians, Chinese, Hebrews or Russians. In other parts of the building may be illustrated lectures or motion pictures. So you see a Settlement has a very busy and varied sort of day's work, and is a good neighbor to the immigrant.

Other Good Neighbors. In addition to the good neighbors mentioned, many other forces assist in the Americanizing of the foreigner. America itself, the streets, the stores, the factories, the public institutions, the work at which he is employed and the conditions under which he toils, all have a marked effect upon the stranger. Those who have studied the matter say that the Jew is developing a better physical type than at home, while the Italian, used to open air peasant life, is running down in stature.

While the immigrant is a stranger in a strange land he is by no means a stranger in a friendless land. America is not only rich in dollars, it is rich in kindness and sympathy. Our fathers were pilgrims and strangers; some of us were ourselves strangers. We should, therefore, try to carry out Christ's story of the good neighbor, and, if we find our immigrant brother in need of help or protection, we should be among the first to have compassion on him.

VIII
GOOD NEIGHBORS AND BAD

"Lead on, O King eternal,

The day of march has come:

Henceforth in fields of conquest

Thy tents shall be our home.

Through days of preparation

Thy grace has made us strong,

And now, O King eternal,

We lift our battle song."

———————————

THE CHURCH. The Protestant church in America is a good neighbor to the immigrant. The trouble is that many immigrants refuse to permit it to be their friend.

We have seen that the chief reason that the church cannot do what it would among the Jews, Russians, Italians and Chinese, the people we are studying, is because these people do not understand that the church in America is different from the church in their home countries. They do not know that American Christianity is a friend of liberty, and is really trying to aid the common people.

When the Irish immigrants came in such multitudes to America they thronged the Catholic Churches. Their church had been their loyal champion in Ireland, and they knew it would be the same friend in America. The same loyalty was shown by the Lutheran to his church when he came from Germany to America.

But the million and more Jews that have flowed into America want to have nothing to do with the church, and the multitudes of Italians, when loyal to any church, belong to the Church of Rome. The Russians are often exiled from home because of the church.

To be the best of good neighbors to these people, it is necessary, first, for the church to know their history. Only in that way can church people understand how the foreigner feels toward the church and how most wisely to approach him.

The Jew and the Church. What does the Jew regard as the cause of the sorrow which has sent him to America? I have seen old Russian Jews stand in front of a Christian church at night, when they thought no eye saw them, and shake their fist at the cross over the door, spit at it, curse it, and go their way. "If," said a Jewish woman, "the Christians want to be friends with the Jews why do they forever preach that the Jews killed Jesus? We know our nation was the cause of His death, but how many Christians have died in the religious wars between themselves?" She laid the persecution of her race at the door of Christianity.

Speaking one day of the religious fervor of an old Hebrew, his daughter said: "Yes, he is religious, but none of the rest of us have any use for it. I think it is through religion that most trouble comes into the world." "Now," she continued, "the best friend I have in America has just gone out angry because when she came in she found a fire in my house, and this is a Jewish fast day. Religion drove us out of Poland with the loss of everything. I believe we would be better off if religion was out of the world." I tried to show her that true Christianity was not guilty of these cruel persecutions of her people, that it was the lack of true Christianity that caused them; yet I doubt if I convinced her.

Even when Jewish children are allowed to attend Christian religious institutions to get them off the streets they are often forewarned. I noticed one day that a boy who sang lustily some of the hymns stopped at the word "Jesus," or else substituted the word, "Moses." "Curley," I said, "why don't you sing the name Jesus?" "My mother told me not to say it or my tongue would turn black," came the prompt reply. Another boy attending our classes reached up and kissed a gold cross that hung on a chain around the neck of one of our workers. He had no sooner done so than he cried across the room to his sister, "It never hurt me." "What did you expect would hurt you?" said the teacher. "My mother told me I could come to class but if I said the name of 'Jesus' it would turn my tongue black, and if I touched the cross, it would kill me, and I didn't believe her." This was especially sad, for the boy said his mother had told him a falsehood.

The Russian and the Church. The Russian dislikes the church. He does not know the Protestant church of America. All he knows is that the church of Russia is at least no friend of liberty. He wants nothing to do with what he considers a similar enemy in America.

The Chinese and the Church. The most devoted Chinese we ever had in our work after he became a Christian, had a similar feeling. His idea of Christianity came from the Catholics of Mexico, who have treated the

Chinese very cruelly. He came to our school because he hoped to learn English and not because he wanted to hear of Christ.

The Italian and the Church. The church in Italy is more or less a political machine. The Italian knows how the Roman church opposed the liberty of Italy and this makes him fear or hate all churches. Great churches in Italy are often found with but a baker's dozen in attendance. The only times on which they are thronged are when a *"festa"* is being held, a festival in honor of some saint.

Brave Christians. Numbers of the immigrants who become Christians are real heroes. The story of the persecutions they suffer would be a surprise to most Christian Americans. The Jewish daily papers sometimes publish the names of the Jewish attendants at Christian meetings that they may incite their Jewish neighbors against them, and the tenement has so bitter a tongue that it often drives the family out of the neighborhood.

Young people who are baptized are mourned for as dead, cast out of their homes, and made practically orphans, and Christian workers must find homes for them. Spies are sent into Christian meetings to secure the names and addresses of Hebrews present, and then letters, or visits, or both, follow. Bibles of young converts are taken from them and burned. While the streets are filled with children with no religious instruction, the whole Ghetto is stirred over one convert to Christ.

One leading Russian revolutionist told me that if he were to come out openly in favor of the Christian church his business would be ruined.

The country founded by men who sought it for liberty of conscience is not a free country to every one and men who have found an asylum here from the oppressor of Europe become in turn oppressors themselves.

The greatest need of all these people is Christ.

The Need of Christ. The non-Christian Chinese are at times cruel and merciless beyond description. Slavery is common among them, women being bought and sold like merchandise. The treatment of little "servant" girls is sometimes so inhuman that they commit suicide. These little girls are bought by the Chinese and then frequently sold by them when 12 or 15 years of age. The picture of two of these little "servant" girls, rescued by the Church of All Nations, appears opposite this page.

How Chinese Babies Ride

Copyright by Underwood & Underwood, New York City

Rescued Slave-Girls (New York City)

One Christmas night a great company of Chinese and their friends had gathered to celebrate the birth of Christ. Chinese women were there who had never before been in a public gathering; bound-feet women were there who are never seen on the streets. The platform was thronged with Chinese children in their quaint, beautiful, and becoming Oriental costumes. The first Christmas was long, long ago. Scripture tells us that on that night a song so full of joy that it startled the shepherds rang through the wintry sky. Poets and other people say that as Christmas time comes round again they can still catch faint echoes of the angels' song. Perhaps the angels still sing it each glad Christmas Eve; anyway, at no other time does a child seem so beautiful and so holy.

When the exercises were over I said a parting word to our guests. One Chinese woman, carrying in her arms a beautiful little baby girl, came up to say good night. "Why, Mrs. Sun," I exclaimed, "I did not know you had a little girl." "Oh," she said, "I hadn't, but Mrs. Wu had one girl and when this baby was born she didn't want it because one girl was enough, so she gave it to me." This in New York on Christmas night, 1911. Can you imagine a Christian mother glad to give away her little girl? The Chinese need Christ.

The Russian needs something other than shorter hours and larger wages. Many of them are seeking the higher things. A Russian pastor told me of making an engagement with one of his hearers at a Russian open air service to discuss and explain Christianity to a Russian in his home. When the night came this Russian revolutionist had gathered a group of his fellows in his tenement quarters and there pastor and men discussed the Christian faith from 8 o'clock in the evening till midnight and would have kept the discussion up all night, could the pastor have remained. Christ and the church are needed by the Russian.

You see that some people have misrepresented our Lord and His church. We must try to right this wrong done the foreigner and we must be patient and loving in doing it. The immigrants are in need of many things— we must endeavor to supply these needs. We must do it for the sake of Christ. We must do it in the name of Christ. We must do it as if our Lord Himself sat weary and thirsty before us and it was given us to hand Him the cup of water. How glad we would be for such an honor!

BAD NEIGHBORS

The Saloon. It is sad to see so many bright Italian boys with their fruit stands and shoe polishing chairs hard by saloon doors. They do not know how great an enemy is pretending to be their friend.

The saloon is a bad neighbor to the immigrant. It wastes his money and his time. It unfits him for work, starves his family and makes them feel ashamed of husband and father. It leads to disease and often to prison, for the saloon is the mother of innumerable crimes. It helps make weak-minded and deformed children and is an evil organization whose destruction has already been determined upon by the truest and best Christian people in our land. For the sake of the immigrant, for the sake of the fair name of America, let us unite to shut its doors and banish it from our country.

Ignorance. Ignorance keeps the immigrant un-American. One who cannot read is at a serious disadvantage. When it is remembered that of the Italians sixty out of one hundred of all those over fourteen years of age who come to America belong to this class, we see the need of the work of night schools to overcome this ignorance. The case is made still worse by the fact that the immigrants crowd together into colonies, as "Little Italy," "Little Russia," and "the Ghetto," where the English language is not spoken and there are no broadening American influences.

Injurious Employment. The work in which the immigrant is generally employed helps keep him un-American. He has no opportunity to know America or to know Americans. Much of the work is wearying and disheartening. Men bound for the coal mines are packed in cars and hurried away, often through the night, to the distant coal fields; underground all day and sleeping in wretched quarters above ground at night, they have little opportunity to see or know anything of their adopted land. I stepped up to a stone house alongside a railroad excavation in the country part of Connecticut once to have a look at the occupants. There were two floors in the old tumble-down house and both were packed with mattresses and makeshifts for beds until practically the whole floor space was covered. It was a wet day and all the men were crowded indoors. A handsome young fellow lay sick on one of the mattresses. I put my head in the door and said: "*Io parlo un poco Italiano ma non bene.*" "I speak a little Italian, but not well." Immediately there was a laugh, probably at the "not well," and they rose to greet me as courteously as if all were trained gentlemen. The sick boy began to talk and the group was friendly with me in a moment.

The day will come when we shall find that these people can do something other than dig ditches and mix concrete. The Italians who are now employed as our hewers of wood and drawers of water, are of the race of painters and sculptors and silk makers of earlier days.

We must help the immigrant to overcome his bad neighbors, and to know who are his true friends.

IX
NEIGHBORS TO THE WORLD

For lo, there breaks a yet more glorious day;

The saints triumphant rise in bright array;

The King of glory passes on His way.

From earth's wide bounds, from ocean's farthest coast,

Through gates of pearl streams in the countless host,

Singing to Father, Son and Holy Ghost,

"Hallelujah, Hallelujah!"

THOSE WHO GO BACK. "Do these immigrants ever go back home?" asks some one. "If I went away from home and made my fortune I would want to go back home to spend it."

I am glad to hear that question and some of you may be surprised at the answer.

We have all heard of the incoming immigrant army, and small wonder when we know that in some years it numbers over a million human beings. But we have heard little about the returning army. How large is it? How many of our immigrant neighbors prefer to spend their savings at home? How many go home because fortune has not smiled upon them in America, or because their mothers write, "I am getting old and it is very lonesome with my son far across the sea"?

Let us lay on the table nine, bright, new, copper pennies. Now suppose each penny represents one hundred thousand immigrants. Then the nine pennies would represent nine times one hundred thousand, or the nine hundred thousand immigrants that landed in 1911. Since almost three hundred thousand immigrants went back home in 1911 how many of these nine pennies shall we have to remove to show the actual immigrant increase for that year?

For 1908 we would have to use eight pennies to represent those who came, and to remove six of these pennies to represent the numbers that returned home that year.

I am sure this will surprise some of you. You did not know so great a multitude returned to Italy, or Russia, or elsewhere, yet every year anywhere from two hundred thousand to six hundred thousand leave our shores for home. That makes us feel the truth of the song we all know,

"Be it ever so humble,

There's no place like home."

Influence of the Returned Immigrant. What effect has this home-coming multitude upon towns and villages all over the world?

When Stefano came to America he could neither read nor write. One day a friend said, "I know a church where Italians are taught to read free of all expense." Stefano was sending money home to his mother each month, so he was glad to know of a free school. One night the leader of the school said, "We shall have a short session to-night because we are to have a prayer-meeting after school." Stefano and fifty other young Italians remained for the prayer-meeting. At home Stefano had ceased going to church after he had been confirmed, except sometimes on feast days. He remained to the prayer-meeting, not because he wanted to but because all the others stayed. He listened with great attention to the speaker; he had never heard such an earnest address as the pastor gave that night. It seemed as if some one must have told the preacher all about him. All through the week he thought of the prayer-meeting and after he had attended a few times more he came to the preaching service on Sundays, and then Stefano became converted.

When he returned home he was on fire with the new religion he had found. His heart was full of love for everybody. But he was saddened when he saw how little the people of his village knew about God. One night he determined to tell them how he had found Christ in America, and so he called them together in his mother's home and told his story. When he had finished what was his surprise and delight to have three other men rise and tell how they had found the same Christ in golden America.

Every one was interested. The villagers said, "Some of these men were bad men when they went away; they are now good men." You will be glad to know that whole villages in Sicily have become Protestant and Christian by the preaching of just such returned immigrants as Stefano. Last year eighteen Protestant Churches of one denomination were founded in Sicily by returned immigrants converted in America.

This shows us the wonderful opportunity we have of being a good neighbor to one part of the world by being good neighbors to the Italians who live near us.

What has caused so old and conservative a nation as China to change to a republic? The leaders of this revolution are Christian men. If we asked them they would say, "We saw that the cities and towns and schools and churches and men and women and children of Christian lands were different from those of China. We believe the reason they are better is because they know Christ and are following Him."

We have helped China by being a good neighbor to the Chinese who lived among us.

A few weeks ago a Russian school-teacher attended a preaching service in my church. After the Russian pastor had finished preaching the school-teacher sought him out and said: "I had fifty young men in my class in the Russian village where I taught. I told these scholars all I knew about God but I could not tell them much, I knew so little myself. I determined to know more so I visited the most celebrated monasteries in Russia in order to find out about God, but I didn't find God in the monasteries. At the great monastery of Kieff after talking for hours with the abbot he said, 'You are too good a man to come in here. Go back into the world, and somewhere there you will find God.' I found him this morning as I listened to the sermon. Now I shall go back to Russia and tell the men of my village of the God who now speaks to my heart."

We shall help the Russian Empire by being a good neighbor to these subjects of the Czar.

America is to-day the greatest mission field on earth. It is not this because of the vast number of foreigners who remain and make it their home; it is such because of the vast human river that flows back to its source. In a barren desert tract in the West, where sage brush and cactus are the only vegetation, the desert blossoms when the rivers of irrigation are let in. So does this returning human flood bring hope and new life to wornout and often hopeless civilizations.

Here lie the responsibility and privilege of America. Through school and settlement and church and a myriad other institutions and influences we must make these Old World brothers and sisters feel that they have found in the New World more tender and loving neighbors than those they left behind; we must show them that accepting our science and education, our ways of farming, and mining and manufacturing, is not enough, although these have had much to do with our greatness. Queen Victoria when asked the source of England's greatness, pointed to the Bible. It was a true answer. It is being humble followers of Christ that makes us fit leaders of these foreigners, and sends them back fit to be leaders in their turn.

If we are helpful, loving Christian neighbors to these immigrants we shall set in motion waves of Christian faith and hope and love that, like the tides, will sweep around the world and break in benediction on every Old World shore.

Milton Keynes UK
Ingram Content Group UK Ltd.
UKHW010838190424
441445UK00004B/310